Man with Farm Seeks Woman with Tractor

Man with Farm Seeks Woman with Tractor

THE BEST AND WORST PERSONAL ADS OF ALL TIME

LAURA SCHAEFER

THUNDER'S MOUTH PRESS
NEW YORK

Man with Farm Seeks Woman with Tractor
The Best and Worst Personal Ads of All Time

Published by
Thunder's Mouth Press
An Imprint of Avalon Publishing Group Inc.
245 West 17th St., 11th Floor
New York, NY 10011

AVALON
publishing group incorporated

Library of Congress Cataloging-in-Publication Data is available.

ISBN 1-56025-686-9

9 8 7 6 5 4 3 2 1

Book design by Maria Elias
Printed in the United States of America
Distributed by Publishers Group West

CONTENTS

OVERVIEW

FOR MILLIONS OF PEOPLE, the most compelling online site isn't an auction or a bookseller. It's not a place to buy stock or get the news. It's an application that's a little more, well, personal. Hopefuls subscribe each week in droves to dating sites such as Match.com and Yahoo Personals, and thousands more take a free look at the "goods" every day. We've always appreciated personals ads for their sheer daring and occasional hilarity . . . but who knew they would ever be this mainstream? Personal ads cross our desks each day on computer screens and in newspapers. They appear on the margins of our favorite Web sites and on the last page of alumni magazines. There are a million attractive, wealthy people out there who enjoy long walks on the beach just waiting to fall in love with you.

Most folks think that personals were an invention of the 1960s and are still in a relative period of adolescence. The truth, however, is far more interesting. It's hard to believe, but we had some ad-happy ancestors. Even the Victorians published the occasional date search. In 1853, for example, a woman named Sophie was looking for Mr. Right: "He must be six feet in height, a fine figure, but not at all fleshy, an intellectual and benevolent countenance, a well shaped head and by no means a large foot."

Personal ads have been around for almost three hundred

years, entertaining readers and linking hopeless romantics ever since a brave woman in Manchester, England, dared to take out the first notice for a husband in 1727.

Because they have always been fun to read, interesting personals were often widely reprinted in the early days as filler by large newspapers, while some publications simply placed the notices on their classified page with little fanfare in a "matrimonial" category near miscellaneous notices for psychics and miracle cures. The sprinkling of personal ads before the mid-1800s gave way to a deluge of "matrimonial papers" during the last quarter of the nineteenth century. These publications, sent for through the mail, contained pages of hopeful brides and bridegrooms. Information about the specific content of bank accounts as well as detailed physical descriptions were common in the ads. In the United States, *The Wedding Bell* and *The Correspondent* circulated among the romantic and curious. In the UK, the twenty-four-page *Matrimonial Herald* and *Fashionable Marriage Gazette* claimed to serve the rich and royal aristocracy, and *The Matrimonial News* boasted three hundred ads per week, most advertisers good-looking and "in good circumstances."

From the infamous *Times* of London agony column of the nineteenth century to the myriad dating Web sites active today, it seems that just about everybody has advertised for love at some point, whether it be a coworker in the next cubicle over or your great-great-grandmother. With little patience for cupid, folks from centuries past right up until now have embraced the marketplace. Perhaps we can't yet buy love, but good ad space is probably the next best thing.

In the 1960s, personals content suddenly shifted from marriage to sex and dating. Soon, niche publications filled with ads from people freed in the sexual revolution, seeking self-actualization and new "adventures." The acronym space-saving system developed as a code for those "in the know." The personals came of age. Now personal ads are one of the most profitable Web applications of all, with multitudes of matchmaking sites taking ads into the mainstream.

In all that time, millions of personal ads have been written and pored over. Only a few, however, stand out for their humor, their uniqueness, or their poignancy. Some are just plain strange, a few are almost poetic, others too clever for their own good. We all read personal ads, but never before has a collection like this been assembled from so many decades past. Here you have it—the best and worst personals from three centuries of the hopeful and the hopeless, the bitter and the sweet, the lovely and the lonely. It's all in these pages, from penniless princesses to kinky convicts.

CHAPTER ONE

I SAW YOU . . .

NOTHING COULD BE more thrilling than to see your description in black and white after a chance encounter with an attractive stranger. These ads are especially evocative, leaving us to wonder if the two people in question ever met again . . . over a headless chicken?

WHEREAS, ON SATURDAY last, a lady, genteelly dressed, was seen to lead a string of beautiful stone-horses through Edmonton, Tottenham, and Newington—this is to acquaint her, that if she is disengaged and inclinable to marry, a gentleman who was on that occasion is desirous of making honorable proposals to her; in which state if he be not so happy as to please, he will readily purchase the whole string for her satisfaction.

— *March 30, 1748,* General Advertiser *(England).*
Reprinted December 27, 1870,
Brooklyn Daily Eagle

A CARD.—If the Lady who a Gentleman handed into her carriage from Covent Garden Theatre, on Wednesday, the third of this month, will oblige the Advertiser with a one to Z.Z., Spring Garden Coffee House, saying if married or single, she will quiet the mind of a young Nobleman, who had tried, but in vain, to find the Lady. The carriage was ordered to Bond Street. The Lady may depend on honour and secrecy. Nothing but the most honourable interview is intended. The Lady was in mourning, and sufficiently clothed to distinguish her for possessing every virtue and charm that man could desire in a female that he would make choice of for a Wife. Deception will be detected, as the Lady's person can never be forgot.

—*December 18, 1800,*
The Times *(London)*

IF THE GENTLEMAN (supposed a Foreigner) who kindly took a YOUNG LADY from No. 13, Charlotte-street, Rathbone-Place, to Bristol, the beginning of September last, will appoint a Place and Time of Meeting with the Advertiser, whose discretion and secrecy may be relied upon, it may be attended with real benefit to the young Lady. Direct to D.G., at John's Coffee-house, Cornhill.

—December 31, 1801,
The Times *(London)*

MY OWN DEAR ALICE—OFT SINCE LAST I saw you have I at most and even gazed at the favorite window where my heart was made glad by your own happy smiles. But my Alice was not there, and I could only (which I did) dream of your whereabouts. Oh, when shall I see you? I shall be at the Point four weeks awaiting orders. Write at once and think of yours.
GEORGE

— July 22, 1857,
The New York Times

A CARD.—H.J. A. presents his most respectful compliments to the Catholic Widow Lady, residing near London-Bridge, and earnestly requests a speedy interview. Should this meet the Lady's, or any of the family's eyes, it is for obvious reasons desired that this may meet the attention which the nearest relationship pleads for. An answer, addressed to the Blossoms Inn, Lawrence-lane, Cheapside, will be attended to.

—September 4, 1804,
The Times *(London)*

A LADY WHO passed a Gentleman on Monday, the 17th of this month in Hart-street, Blooms-bury, about 3 o'clock in the afternoon, without speaking to him, is anxious for an opportunity of seeing him again, any time after the 7th of January.

—December 25, 1810,
The Times *(London)*

IF THE GENTLEMAN who met a LADY in Gracechurch-street, on the evening of the 9th of November last, and walked with her to the lower end of Bishopgate-street, and then waited till her return, and then accompanied her into the City, will be at the exact spot where he waited for her, at 8 o'clock on Wednesday and Thursday next, she will meet him, having something of importance to communicate.

—*September 10, 1811,*
The Times *(London)*

WILL EITHER OR BOTH of the young ladies who crossed Fulton Ferry on Sunday, the 16th, about 2 1/2 o'clock, and met two gentlemen by Fulton Market, have any objection to meeting two old friends? If not, address James, Herald Office.

—The New York Herald. *Reprinted February 23, 1862,* The New York Times

A MIDDLE-SIZED GENTEEL gentleman, supposed to be of the age of twenty-five or thereabouts, of a handsome, cheerful countenance, a widish mouth with very fine teeth, looked like a clergyman, and was chiefly in company with a very young officer at Ranelagh on Friday. If the said gentleman is really of the Church of England, and is a single man, and has no objection to an agreeable companion for life of a pious and virtuous disposition, not much turned of thirty, and who is in possession of a very handsome jointure, by directing a line to M.A. at Jack's Coffee House, may hear of further particulars.

—Reprinted December 10, 1868,
"Old Newspapers," Brooklyn Daily Eagle

LADY WHOSE CAR ticket was refused by conductor on S. Meridian car, Friday, June 20 at 7 a.m. wishes to communicate with gentleman who witnessed the refusal. DRexel 5056.

—June 26, 1924,
Indianapolis Star

WILL THE GENTLEMAN WHO KINDLY assisted me up from the ground when I fell off the street car and took me to my daughter's house at 837 William Ave. Dec. 6th, 1915, Kindly communicate with the undersigned, Mrs. E. J. Thomas. 422 Hannatyne Avenue.

—August 20, 1920,
The Manitoba Free Press *(Canada)*

TRACY FROM HONG KONG 1/1/04 at LamHoa-Thuan on Irving Street. You: so nice, sweet, and funny, that I'd love to meet again. Perhaps a lunch of headless chicken?

—*February 18, 2004,*
San Francisco Bay Guardian

CHAPTER TWO

DESPERATE
(SIZE, AGE, BEAUTY NO OBJECT)

FOR EVERY PERSONAL advertisement listing a set of impossible standards, there is another one out there looking for, well, *anybody*. Funny and unpretentious, these desperate ads were written by everyone from farmers and down-and-out royalty to firmly closeted gay men and lonely soldiers.

ANY GAL WHAT'S got a cow, a good feather bed, with comfortable fixings, 500 dollars in hard pewter, one that has had the measles and understands tending children, can find a customer for life by writing a small billet box, addressed Z.Q. and stick it in a crack of Uncle Ebenezer's barn, back side of the hen pen.

—American newspaper. Reprinted 1840,
The Times *(London)*

MATRIMONY. A PIOUS and experienced farmer, 32 years of age, six feet high and Possessed of Good Property is desirous to meet with a lady that is Competent to manage Dairy and is Possessed of 100£ or more and will make herself Extra Useful. Size, Age, and Beauty no object.

—October 16, 1840,
The Times *(London)*

ANY GAL WHAT'S got a bed, coffee pot, and skillit; knows how to cut out britches, can make a huntin' shirt, and knows how to take care of children, can have my services until death parts both of us.

—November 24, 1855,
The Provincial Freeman *(Canada).*
Reprinted from Batesville News *(Arkansas)*
(Courtesy Accessible Archives, www.accessible.com)

MIDDLE-AGED WIDOWER, tall, good-looking, kind, sympathetic, nice home, sadly needs woman's care; has $30,000; would marry soon. Address Mr. Milton, box 675, Chicago, Ill.

—December 29, 1901,
The Atlanta Constitution

PENNILESS AND HOMELESS—Well-known Prince and Princess (Russian), with five very young children and aged relative, absolutely stranded in London; will any one OFFER ACCOMMODATION anywhere? A small fund being arranged for food by friends; any kind of help most gratefully accepted.

—British newspaper.
Reprinted May 29, 1921, "The New Agony,"
The New York Times

YONGE STREET. AM 28, 5 feet 4, weight 132, live over a nice store on Yonge Street with other chums. Would break off from them if I could get a good Sunday School teacher or Christian widow to relieve my monotony. Have pity on me, dear girls.

—May 14, 1892,
Canadian Matrimonial News

WANTED, BY AN industrious young man of thirty years of age, of temperate habits, who neither uses tobacco, drinks whisky, nor swears, a partner for life, with five or ten thousand dollars. Of course, a lady preferred. For particulars, address M., Geneva, N.Y.

—June 4, 1857, The National Era, #11, no. 544, p. 91 (Courtesy Accessible Archives, www.accessible.com)

FRIENDLESS SOLDIER WOULD much like some nice girl to write to him. Being without friends feels awful lonely, and would much appreciate cheerful letters. (Box A. 99).

—British newspaper. Reprinted September 19, 1916, The Indiana Evening Gazette (Pennsylvania)

THE PARENTS OF a young lady, aged 21, handsome, well educated, and possessing 4,300 francs per annum, but affected by St. Vitus's dance, offer to unite her to a doctor from 40 to 45 years old, who will pay her incessant attention.

— January 30, 1856,
Manchester Guardian *(England)*

TWO ROYAL PRINCESSES, sisters, aged 23 and 26, desire friendship and eventually marriage, after mutual tests, with English or American gentlemen, who must be young, wealthy, and handsome. No upstarts or new-rich need apply. The princesses are accomplished but very poor. A meeting could be arranged for August. Post Office Box 31.

—September 1922,
The Indianapolis Star Tribune

TO WHOM IT May Concern: I have received from reliable sources that *Ames Daily Tribune* is a reliable paper and I am pleading to you to do me a favor. Well, to get down to facts, I am a lonesome GI overseas, and stationed with the 49th Ordnance M.M. company. I'm in charge of classification and reclamation, attached to supply section and all I have to do is work, eat and sleep. My object in writing this letter is to raise my morale by receiving more mail. Would you please publish this ad in your want ad section?: "WANTED: MORE MAIL Lonesome GI overseas wishes to receive more mail, and promises to answer all letters received. Age 19. Address as follows: Pfc. H. N. Barbian, 16241038, 49th Ord. M.M. Cc., APO 547, c/o P. M., San Francisco, Calif."

Will gladly pay bill for running this ad for three days if sent to my address.

—*1946,* The Ames Daily Tribune *(Iowa)*

WILL WELCOME ALL letters from anyone who cares
to write.

Would like to hear from anyone, anywhere.

Will write anyone who writes me.

Will reply to all male mail, any age or race.

Will respond to males within a radius of 100 miles.

Wishes correspondence with other gay men.

—1968. Reprinted in The Male Swinger:
The Rise and Fall of Gay Culture *by Daniel
Harris, New York: Hyperion, 1997, p. 278.*

The middle aged widower who advertised three weeks ago is still a candidate for matrimony.

—*Reprinted October 18, 1885,*
"The Wife Market," Brooklyn Daily Eagle

CHAPTER THREE

SO I HAVE THIS FRIEND . . .

ADVERTISING ON BEHALF of a friend didn't start a couple years ago with the advent of GreatBoyfriends.com. No, it seems matchmaking via personal ad was begun long ago by folks willing to cast the net a little wider than the traditional dinner party when it came to pairing off their lovelorn pals. And with good results. These personals avoid the awkward self-promotion that plagues the average notice. Looking for love? Put your most eloquent friends to work on your personal.

MATRIMONY—THE FRIEND of a Gentleman (a Bachelor), about 26, who is a Man of good property, agreeable person, and in an old-established profitable Business in one of the best and most fashionable streets at the West-end of the Town, wishes to see him made happy by an honorable union with an amiable Female of good education, pleasing manners, and some property. This Advertisement is inserted by his friend without his knowledge, by which means he hopes to introduce a Lady to his wishes, and prevent the possibility of prejudice on his part by this too common channel of information. Any Lady (Widow or Spinster) not exceeding 30 years of age, who may answer this Advertisement (not out of curiosity only), may depend on secrecy, and the greatest honor and most respectable reference, by addressing a line to Mr. Thomas Price, to be left at the Printing-office, Grocer's Hall-court, Poultry.

—December 15, 1801,
The Times *(London)*

THE FRIENDS OF AN ENGLISH YOUNG LADY—
Wish to find a suitable partner for her in marriage.
She is but nineteen, has fair hair, blue eyes, bright,
clear complexion, fine teeth, and is a beautiful and
engaging person. She has a superior education in
languages and music, and with a well stored mind,
is lively, agreeable, affectionate, and confiding.
These qualities are her wealth. An interview can be
obtained with her about the 10th of December on
her return from the country, where all answers will
be sent to her. Address (with entire confidence, as
no interference will be made, nor the correspondence seen by any other person) L.L.L., Post-
Office, New York.

—December 1855,
The New York Times

HE HAS AN estate of upwards £4,000 a year, but requires £20,000 to pay off old family encumbrances (a larger sum would be more acceptable if the lady possessed it) and leave his estate free. This advertisement is real bona fida, and ought to be important to any amiable lady desirous to marry a worthy, kind-hearted nobleman who would make her happy. He has a power to settle £1,000 a year on her for life. His lordship is entirely unaware of the publication of this advertisement, which is the act of a sincere old friend and well-wisher, who knows his wishes on the subject, and all his circumstances. Address, W. M. under cover to the editor M. N., 282 strand, London.

— The Matrimonial News *(England)*.
Reprinted June 21, 1873,
The Denton Journal *(Maryland)*

CHAPTER FOUR

JUST PLAIN STRANGE . . .

SOME PERSONAL ADS are so startling they defy explanation. With mention of everything from glass eyes and preserved jars of meat to healed boils and one-legged runaway wives, these personal ads are enough to open your eyes a little wider when the morning coffee just isn't doing the trick.

ELIZA, YOU CAN return to the house. The boil on my nose is gone.

—*French newspaper. Reprinted April 1873,*
Godey's Lady's Book (Philadelphia)
(Courtesy Accessible Archives, www.accessible.com)

TO STIMULATE MATRIMONY

BERLIN—POSSESSION of 75 jars of preserved meats was set forth as an inducement by a young man advertising in the Lorracher Blatt. The young aspirant included among his personal charms and qualifications, ability and willingness to help with the housework.

— *November 19, 1922,*
The Charleston Daily Mail

RUN AWAY LAST night, my wife, Bridget Coole. She is a tight neat body, and has lost one leg. She was seen riding behind the priest of the parish through Fermoy: and, as we never was married, I will pay no debt that she does not contract. She lisps with one tooth, and is always talking about faries, and is of no use but to the owner. —Phelim Coole, his X mark.

—*December 5, 1832,*
The Times *(London)*

An advertisement in the Journal of Paris, for a lost dog, has too much peculiarity to be lost itself.—It says:

POOR FACORI IS neither very young nor very handsome; but very good and very affectionate. The advertiser loved him much, and much regrets him. Let the person who has taken or found Favori, despair of gaining his attachment. No; he will cry; he will groan; he will lose his appetite; he will never forget his former mistress: and any one being hard-hearted enough to detain him, if there remains to this unhappy little animal fifteen or twenty days of life, it is the utmost.

This translation is literal; we really hope that so tender a pair may not long be separated.

—July 25, 1800,
The Times *(London)*

HELP, PLEASE CATCH me before my boobs start to sag. I wasn't able to respond to your ad in time. We may be what we're both looking for. Please call! 45768.

— February 14, 2004,
Chicago Reader

TO UGLY GENTLEMEN.—Magdalena aged 28, of prepossessing appearance, and loving, confiding disposition, wishing for a husband described as above.—Must be interesting and refined. No cold-hearted gentlemen need apply, whatever may be his position or fortune. The Editor has address.

—The Matrimonial News *(England).*
Reprinted June 21, 1873,
The Denton Journal *(Maryland)*

YOUNG MAN, MODERATE circumstances and who has glass eye, would like to form the acquaintance of young girl who also has a glass eye or some other deformity not more severe; object, matrimony. Address—.

— August 17, 1903,
The Coshocton Daily Age *(Ohio)*

NUDIST WM 32, in shape fitness buff. Looking to meet other in shape male nudists, any age, to hang out and spend some nude time together. Watching TV, surfing 'net, sunning in the summer, nude travel, etc. Father/son family nudists also welcome!

— *February 14, 2004*,
Chicago Reader

ADVANTAGEOUS PROPOSAL:

A GENTLEMAN ADVANCED in years, who is possessed of a considerable fortune, the apparent heir to which (a graceless nephew) has treated him in a manner utterly unpardonable, would be glad to enter into the connubial fate with a healthy pregnant young widow of a reputation unsullied; however contracted her sphere in life be. The utmost secrecy and honour may be relied on, and by inclosing her name and address to X.Y.Z. under cover to the Printer, she will be immediately waited on by the Advertiser. N.B. No notice whatever will be taken of anonymous Letters.

—The Hibernian Telegraph *(Ireland).*
Reprinted September 8, 1800,
The Times *(London)*

KINGSTON. I AM a dear little duck of a girl, father was a U.E.L. and has lots of property for me, as I am the only chick. I am 24, and weigh 133, 4 feet 9. Write to me at once, boys, as I believe in annexation.

—*May 14, 1892,*
Canadian Matrimonial News

A HUSBAND'S ADVERTISEMENT

THE HUDDERSFIELD MAGISTRATES had before them an amusing matrimonial case, the complainant being a Mrs. Catherine Horne. She stated that she had been unhappy since a fortnight after her marriage, nine years ago. Among the charges of cruelty made against her husband was that on one occasion he advertised her in a local paper as follows: "Strayed or stolen from Dungeon Nersery a chestnut mare, 17 hands, good in action. Any one returning same will be handsomely rewarded; detainer prosecuted."— Mrs. Horne was granted a separation.

—April 1, 1900,
News of the World *(England)*

SAN QUENTIN CONVICT. I am 26 years old, Hawaiian, doing time for robbery. I'd dig hearing from chicks that aren't hung up on middle class Amer. type life! If you're into the communal organic bag, that's outasite. Saying what you think and feel is beautiful. Don't know anyone from Ca. as I got busted right after coming from Hawaii, so it'll be an experience for me too. Will answer all. Peace!

—1971,
The Los Angeles Free Press

COUNT SARSFIELD, LORD Lucan, descendant of the royal branches of Lorraine and Capet, and other sovereigns of Europe, wishes to contract an alliance with a lady capable from her rank and talents of supporting the dignity and titles which an alliance so honorable would confer to her.

—Unidentified source, 1818.
Reprinted in The Mating Trade *by Bob Mullan,*
Boston: Routledge & Kegan Paul, 1984, p. 163.

MONSTER SEEKS DAMSEL Hungry Beastie desires voluptuous damsel for chasing about, carrying off and general "distressing." Beastie is passionate and gentle. Would love to have YOU for dinner!

—February 18, 2004,
The Independent Weekly *(Durham, North Carolina)*

ON MARRIAGE

HAPPY RELIEF FOR Young Men from the effects of Errors and Abuses in early life. Manhood restored. Impediments to marriage removed. New method of treatment. New and remarkable remedies. Books and circulars sent free in sealed envelopes. Address Howard Association, No. 9, South Ninth St, Philadelphia, PA.—an Institution have a high reputation for honorable conduct and professional skill.

—September 4, 1873,
Colorado Daily Chieftan

The following curious matrimonial advertisement recently appeared in a Tokyo, Japan, paper:

I AM A BEAUTIFUL woman. My abundant undulating hair envelopes me as a cloud. Supple as a willow is my waist. Soft and brilliant is my visage as the satin of the flowers. I am endowed with wealth sufficient to saunter through life hand in hand with my beloved. Were I to meet a gracious lord, kindly, intelligent, well educated and of good taste, I would unite myself with him for life, and later share with him the pleasure of being laid to rest, eternal in a tomb of pink marble.

—*Japanese newspaper. Reprinted October 2, 1901*
Nebraska State Journal

AS ONLY LIKE and like can be enduringly happy, I desire a wife who has a similar physical affliction. Young woman who has one leg shorter than the other preferred. Artificial leg not excluded. Give age, description and a history of defect.

—German newspaper. Reprinted September 18, 1912, "Odd Ads in German Paper: Those Matrimonially Inclined Frankly State Their Desires in Big Display Type," Evening Post *(Frederick, Maryland)*

CHAPTER FIVE

A LITTLE BITTER, ARE WE?

DISTRESSED PERSONALS

NOT EVERY PERSONAL ad out there is full of romance and happy-go-lucky hopefulness. Despite the almost disturbing amount of cheerful people smiling out from the pages of AnyDatingSite.com, the story of personal ads contains a good amount of bitterness, revenge, and pleading. While one woman warns others away from her ne'er-do-well husband, plenty of others make entreaties to the ne'er-do-wells themselves. Finally, an increasingly common type of ad spends more time on the negatives, leaving everyone with the clear understanding that this advertiser isn't PUTTING UP with %@* ANYMORE!

YOU WON MY heart, to break it, then leave me, friendless. I live in the past—your precious promises. Personal necessity makes me desperate; for God's sake send me something immediately or anxiety will kill me and all will be known. M.G.

—*January 11, 1869,*
The New York Times

THOMAS HUTCHINS HAS advertised, that I have absented my self from his bed and board, and forbid all persons trusting me on his account, and cautioned all persons against making me any payment on his account. I now advertise the public, that the same THOMAS HUTCHINS came as a fortune-teller into this town about a year ago, with a recommendation, which, with some artful falsehoods, induced me to marry him. Of the four wives he had before me, the last he quarelled away; how the other three came by their deaths, he can best inform the public; but I caution all widows or maidens against marrying him, be their desire for matrimony ever so strong. Should he make his advances under a feigned name, they may look out for a little, strutting, talkative, feeble, meagre, hatchet-faced fellow, with spindle shanks, and a little warped in the back. "East Windsor, May 22, 1807. THANKFUL HUTCHINS."

—The Connecticut Courant.
Reprinted by The Times *(London)*

TO M—AM—E. "Forget" you? By Heaven I cannot! Engraven on my soul is your memory, in deepest characters, which time vainly will endeavour to efface, contracted as now must be its span, since without one remonstrance, one expostulation, you can resolve for ever to forget me. Wherefore, then, often warned, persist in exciting a reluctant, indeed, but never more unfeigned, sensibility, only to wound it? DO I DESERVE THIS? Is it generous? Is it equitable? But severe no longer, welcome now, is the mandate of authority, enjoining oblivion of ORL—O.

—June 16, 1804,
The Times *(London)*

G.B.—IF EVERY manly feeling is not extinct in you, you will return directly. It is false shame to leave a woman to combat difficulties that you could not withstand. You are vilified, as if you were a bad man, and that by persons whose indulgence you might expect. Your presence may reverse what has been done. It will relieve those who love you, from distress the most unutterable.

—April 27, 1818,
The Times *(London)*

MOSS ROSE.—The Lady who clandestinely left her home on the 1st of May is most earnestly implored to RETURN immediately, or to write to "Highlander," whom she so cruelly deceived on the evening of Wednesday. Feelings of the warmest affection, saddened, alas! by intense grief, incite this announce.

—May 12, 1851,
The Times *(London)*

MRS._____N.–Your note has been received. It is evasive, cold, and cruel. It is incredible that you should be watched and coerced; if so, come at once to the man who is now fully prepared to be satisfactorily yours only, and for life. What accursed spirit holds you in thralldom, and can influence you to abandon your child and husband? In wretchedness he appeals to you against this influence. Let the feelings of your own good heart prevail. RETURN, if but for a few days, to your home, and confer with your husband. Nothing shall be done to mar your comfort or ease, but do not, for the will of others, sacrifice the peace of mind and health of the man you have professed to love above all others. Your husband, A.F.

—*October 29, 1851,*
The Times *(London)*

HOPE.—BY that pure love I have struggled to preserve, with every effort of my soul; by that bitter cup you have given, and I drank to the dregs—by those ties no man can sever—by promises made to those now no more—I will see you. Be true to yourself and to me. Oh! M—y! M—y! I would save you the pangs of error—God forbid of crime—and though the passion, jealousy, hate and madness you have excited—be scorned and denied—when the serpent you foster is wearied—yea, even then—here is your haven, when all forsake.

God protect you.—D—.

—*November 1, 1855,*
The Times *(London)*

S.M.U.—YOU little rogue, did you keep me waiting so long on Friday night and then not come, to punish me for the previous evening? I waited an hour, and then returned to the Viper's, but of course, did not go in. Why, too, did you not come on Saturday? You know full well how I wanted to see you. Do write to S.M.J.

—*October 31, 1856,*
The Times *(London)*

CHAPTER SIX

AW, HOW SWEET . . .

SOME PERSONAL ADS warm the heart by being just plain sincere, clever, or earnest. With everything from a church door posting to a grateful American, this chapter stretches our perceptions of just what a little personal ad can accomplish.

MATRIMONY—A FOREIGN Merchant, 33 years of age, who is permanently settled at Manchester, and well acquainted with the language, and manners, and customs of English society, but whose business avocations have prevented him forming much acquaintance with the female sex, respectfully makes known to any accomplished and independent lady that in the advertiser she will meet a domesticated, amiable, and gentlemanly partner for life: one who wishes for the comfort of an English fireside. The advertiser's intentions being most honourable, any lady favoring him with a reply, which must be very explicit, may depend upon the most inviolable secrecy being preserved. Means are taken to prevent imposition being practiced.— Address Alpha, Box 860, Post-office, Manchester.

—February 8 and 15, 1851,
Manchester Guardian *(England)*

MARRIAGE. THE ADVERTISER, a young man, aged 20, (a Catholic), respectably connected, and of mild and exceedingly regular habits, is desirous of forming a Matrimonial Alliance with any virtuous and healthy young lady, of mild disposition, and not older than himself. References can be given if required, and it is hoped none will apply but in a spirit of truth and sincerity.—Address, with particulars, to E.S., Post Office, Preston, Lancashire.—The most honourable confidence may be relied upon.

— April 6, 1851,
News of the World *(England)*

MATRIMONY—THE ADVERTISER, who has been much abroad, has no relations, feels lonely, and possesses a good round sum for the matrimonial cash-box, wishes to find a single or widow lady in a similar position, having a wish to marry. As to personal attractions, an interview is best to satisfy. He is genteel, of studious habits, gentle temper, neat in dress, and fond of traveling. Not exact as to age. Would prefer a plain, neat lady, rather than a dashy person.—All letters will be attended to in four days after received.—Address to R. Daron, 193, Bishopsgate-street Withour, London.

—September 28, 1851,
News of the World *(England)*

MATRIMONY.—A YOUNG Gentleman, aged 24, just returned to England, after an absence of several years, finding himself without a home, is desirous of meeting with a partner, to share his fortune, and contribute to his happiness. The lady must be young, cheerful, and well educated. Wealth no object.—Address Q 63, at the printer's.

— January 19, 1856,
Manchester Guardian *(England)*

The following notice was distributed at the doors of Edmonton church after a sermon preached by the Rev. Dr. Hawker:

A TRADESMAN, of domestic habits and a retired life, between 30 and 40 years of age, who has been some time in a respectable trade in London, by which he has acquired of this world's goods from 2,000£ to 10,000£; but, from his situation in life, has not had an opportunity of settling himself with a companion of similar habits—(he trusts he will be found of an accommodating dispositions, and determined to make everyone with whom he has to do comfortable to the utmost of his power)—is desirous of meeting with a female of similar habits and circumstances in life, well versed in domestic concerns, good tempered, obliging to her friends, yet not extravagant or given to much company; neat in her appearance— of light complexion; but, above all, having the grace of God in her heart, and believing Jesus Christ to be all in all to poor miserable sinners. The limits of this paper will not admit of any further description; but should this meet the eye of any one influenced by the same spirit that dictated the above, have no doubt of spending the present state in comfort, and the eternal in everlasting happiness.—A line, addressed to A.B.C., 46, Wellington-street, Goswell-street-road, appointing an interview any day in October next, will be attended to with all secrecy.

—*October 5, 1822,*
The Times *(London)*

BIANCHINA.—I AM yours a thousand times more than ever. Remember you may depend upon me. For God's sake write when you can—t'adoro sempre piu. You belong to me.

—*November 23, 1857,*
The Times *(London)*

MATRIMONY—A GENTLEMAN, about 27 years of age, kind and amiable in disposition, is desirous of meeting with a PARTNER for LIFE. The advertiser is engaged in a prosperous business; and trusts that this mode may be the means of bringing him into communication with one of the fair sex similarly disposed, and of respectable family. The strident secrecy may be relied upon.—Address Y28, at the printers'.

—*January 18, 1851,*
Manchester Guardian *(England)*

MATRIMONY—ANSWER FROM E.B. to the ADVERTISEMENT Y28 in last Saturday's Guardian.—The Party replying to the above advertisement will MEET the Gentleman on Monday, at the same place and hour as stated in E.B.'s application.

—*January 26, 1851,*
Manchester Guardian *(England)*

A GRATEFUL AMERICAN.

WHEN THOU HAST EATEN and are full, then shalt thou bless the Lord thy God for the good land which he hath given thee, Deut., CH. 8, V.10.

Having lived through two unforgettable totalitarian regimes in Europe, where I have suffered untold cruel abuse, through the hand of Providence five years have gone since I came to this free and Blessed U.S.A. I have worked for the last four years at the Garden City Plating Mfg. Co. Through this time there has been extended to me and my fellow workers a warm and pleasant welcome feeling through our foreman, Mr. W. Cruetz and especially from the foreman general, Mr. A. Tantillo. That is why I highly appreciate this warm and pleasant welcome, and I thank God for such sympathetic human beings in this wonderful God Blessed America. —A. Waschenko.

—November 24, 1954,
The Traverse City Record *(Michigan)*

ANY MORAL YOUNG men of good standing and respectability can have an opportunity of entering the "holy bonds of matrimony," with some ladies, who have requested us to advertise for them for husbands. The young ladies in question are remarkably handsome, and of the highest respectability. P.S. Don't forget an "X" for our editor.

—December 22, 1854,
Frederick Douglass' Paper (Rochester, New York)
(Courtesy Accessible Archives, www.accessible.com)

REQUIRED, AN EDUCATED Widow, thirteen to fifteen years of age. She should be of good shape, feature, complexion, temper and health, and not suffering from any hereditary disease, daughter of a well-to-do gentleman, and of respectable caste—for an enlightened young Bengal Zimindar ("landlord") of respectable caste and family, accomplished, well-built, and free from every present and idiopathic defects, and in order to encourage widow marriage amongst the nobles and gentries, he is desirous of presenting the bride at the wedding with jewels worth ten thousand rupees.

—Social Reformer (India). Reprinted July 24,
1885, Daily Gleaner (Kingston, Jamaica)

A YOUNG MAN, permanently established in business, with a comfortable house, is sincerely disposed to settle. Communications will be met with delicacy, explicitness, and candour; age 32; person, rather tall; income 180l£; temper, mild; habits, steady.—The Lady must be good looking, affable, and kind, and as for her age and property, they are comparatively unimportant.—Address, post paid, to J. P. Lombard street Post Office. No letters will be received or answered till June 1.

—London Morning Herald. *Reprinted August 1, 1828,* Freedom's Journal *(New York) (Courtesy Accessible Archives, www.accessible.com)*

A YOUNG GENTLEMAN, aged 22, of pleasant appearance, and genteel manners, and who has gone through a regular course of Academical and University education is desirous of forming a MATRIMONIAL UNION with an agreeable and religious disposed Lady, possessed of the matter of two or three thousand pounds. The advertiser is just commencing business on his own account, as a solicitor in a country town, and has an income of 200l£ a year. The highest references of respectability will be given and asked, and the strictest honour and secrecy may be relied on.—Any letter (post paid) addressed to X.Y., and left at the circulating library, 2 Blandford street, will be immediately attended to.

—London Morning Herald. *Reprinted August 1, 1828,* Freedom's Journal *(New York) (Courtesy Accessible Archives, www.accessible.com)*

A YOUNG GENTLEMAN—Of unquestionable respectability, character and habits (lately from the south), who is engaged in the mercantile business downtown, is desirous of corresponding with, or making the acquaintance of, a young lady of good family, who is amiable, pretty, and intelligent, with a view to matrimonial alliance. Believing the great object of life is the attainment of domestic happiness, and that it cannot exist where there is not a congeniality of tastes and dispositions, the advertiser would state that his tastes and habits are such, that his home would be to him the source of all his happiness. Those who can appreciate the honorable motive of the undersigned, may rely on their communications being treated with the most honorable confidence. Address, William T. Sumpter, *Times* Office

—June 3, 1854,
The New York Times

A GENTLEMAN (AMERICAN AGED 27) wishes to correspond with a young lady with a view to matrimony. The gentleman is possessed of moderate means, and of good moral character. The lady must be of irreproachable character, not more than twenty years of age, medium size or under, some pretense to good looks and of an amiable disposition. The writer does not design to form a hasty marriage, of which both would, most probably, repent at leisure, but means this notice as an avenue by which to form an acquaintance first, more serious matters to be considered after the acquaintance has become sufficiently mature. Communications that do not give good evidence of sincerity will be disregarded. Address for one week, WILLIE WILLIS, *Times* Office.

—*April 19, 1858*,
The New York Times

A YOUNG GENTLEMAN (AGE 24), Holding a good situation, down town in a dry goods importing house, (and not wholly dependent upon it) is anxious to form an acquaintance with a young lady of general accomplishments, with a view to matrimonial alliance—a lady well practiced on the piano is preferred, as the advertiser is particularly fond of music. Communications addressed HENRICUS, Times Office, will be treated confidentially.

—*April 19, 1858,*
The New York Times

A YOUNG WEALTHY GENTLEMAN, on visit to this country, would like to make the acquaintance of an accomplished young lady, with a view to matrimony, money no object. He will leave the City for home in a short time, stopping a short season in France, &c. References Exchanged. All notices received by ROBINSON & WILLIAMS, No. 534 Broadway, prepaid with return stamp.

—*April 19, 1858,*
The New York Times

A YOUNG LADY, OF AGREEABLE Personal appearance and very accomplished manners, desires to secure a partner for life. She possesses a fair annual income in her own right, is 18 years of age, can speak three languages, and play on the guitar and piano. Any sincere American gentleman, of moderate means, who can appreciate an affectionate disposition, and a pretty face, with proper fidelity, may address PARISIENNE, this office, for two days.

—*April 23, 1858,*
The New York Times

A STYLISH YOUNG Parisienne, recently arrived, has found herself suddenly thrown out of occupation, and seeks some honorable means of subsistence. She seeks the acquaintance of some sincere American gentleman, of middle age and permanent business, with a view to marriage. The advertiser is an excellent musician and linguist, is of pleasant disposition, and has much personal attraction; is a good houseworker and can make a home cheerful. Address immediately, JULIE, Box No. 130, Times Office.

—October 12, 1861,
The New York Times

A WIDOWER OF MIDDLE AGE, Without family, in good circumstances, well educated and highly respectable, wishes to form a matrimonial alliance with a lady of good social position, of undoubted integrity, tolerably good looking, and having some pecuniary means. The latter would remain under her own control. Any lady fulfilling these conditions and replying in sincerity will meet with the most respectful and honorable attention. Address EDWARD ENFIELD, New York City, Station D, Bible House.

—October 19, 1861,
The New York Times

LOVE, COURTSHIP, AND MARRIAGE COLUMN

NO. 1—Would like to correspond with a fat, comfortable looking lady not over 40 years old, widow preferred.—Taylor T.

NO. 2—Want to meet a blond girl under 20 years, who can cook wash dishes and keep a large house; looks don't go, object matrimony.—Fred D.

NO. 3—Would like to meet good-looking, slim girl, am awful lonely and need the sunshine of some sweet girl to keep me happy.—Chris F.

NO. 4—A young, good looking, rather heavy set fellow of mild disposition and winning ways wants the acquaintance of a swell dame who can wear the rags and do society, must be good talker, sing a little and dance well; object, wedding bells.—Harold B. (Atty.)

NO. 5—Girls, why waste your time in the idle pleasures of single blessedness, when I offer you such an opportunity for a model husband.—Jeff W.

NO. 6—I am dying of loneliness. Won't some girl please respond to this plea. Am fair to look on, of sunny disposition and have had large experience. Call me up, but don't come to the hotel.—John P.

NO. 7—Wanted, a maiden as sweet as the clover blossoms, with cheeks of rosiest hue, with eyes as blue as the vaulted dome of heaven, and lips as red as the cherry in June. I'll be lovingly yours forever.—Brink.

NO. 8—Wanted, to make the acquaintance of loving young lady between 20 and 30 years of age—between 20 preferred—must be beautiful and able to make her own clothes. Object, matrimony.—Harry W.

NO. 9—A timid young man of retiring disposition and rather sickly, wants to meet a young lady who would make a good nurse and respectable looking widow in case I should pass away. —"Buck" S.

—April 21, 1915,
Bismarck Daily Tribune *(North Dakota)*

CHAPTER SEVEN

PICKY, PICKY
PERSONAL AD AS MANIFESTO

HUNDREDS OF YEARS ago, those wealthy enough to afford the ad space could go on for pages about their predilections . . . and several men (most notably an eccentric German baron) availed themselves of the option. Their personal ads carried on with crotchety abandon. Now, boundless cyberspace makes pontificating in a personal ad even easier than ever. Forget the acronyms—putting it all out there is the newest way to scare a potential mate even before the safe lunch date.

A MIDDLE-AGED GENTLEMAN barely turned 50 and as yet unmarried is desirous of altering his condition. He has a good estate, sound constitution and easy temper, and having worn out the follies of youth will be determined by reason in the choice of the lady he intends to make happy. She must be upward of 15 and under 25. Her size must be moderate, her shape natural, her person clean and her countenance pleasing. She must be lively in her humor, but not smart in her conversation; sensible, but utterly unaffected with wit; her temper without extremes, neither too hasty and never sullen. Then she must invariably observe all forms of breeding in public places and mixed company, but may lay them all aside among her acquaintances. She must have no affectation but that of hiding her perfection, which her own sex will forgive and the other more quickly discover. She shall be restrained in nothing, the gentleman having observed that restraint only makes good women bad and bad women worse. In some things perhaps she may be stinted, which is the only method he will take to signify his dislike to any part of her conduct. Any lady whose friends are of opinion (her own opinion will not do) that she is qualified as above and has a mind to dispose of herself may hear of a purchaser by leaving with the printer hereof a letter directed to C.D.

—American advertisement, 1737.
Reprinted August 16, 1894, Trenton Times

SINGLE MIXED RACE FEMALE SEEKS BOYFRIEND—35

Date: 2004-11-19, 9:56AM EST
OKAY. . . . I'M GOING to give this a try although I have to say, I am not very optimistic. First off let me preface by saying I fully expect a barage of low minded insults, perverts, fruitcakes, bi-sexuals, creeps, racists, idiots, retards. There is nothing you can say in your email to upset me, so don't bother. I've heard it all and seen it all. I know that by posting on Craigslist, you open yourself up for all sorts of verbal abuse. But let's get one thing straight: I am a strong, independent woman and I don't tolerate crap from anybody. Understood?

That said, I am looking for a boy friend. Not marriage, not friendship particularly. About me: I am 5'4", 195lbs, I have medium length dark curly hair (naturally), deep brown eyes (been told thats my most amazing feature) and a very light olive complexion. I am half african-america/half european descent. I am considered very attractive by most people I meet. I know I am bit heavy, but trust me I don't look nearly as bad as you are playing through your head. And I don't sit in bed eating oreos, its not like that. I live in Washington Heights. I work in midtown for a large bank as an assistant, I love my job, it has tons of perks. I have a cat. I have a great sense of humour, I am always making jokes. Basically I am a happy person, not a mean, bitter old bag. I like to go clubbing, dancing. I drink, I don't smoke (anything). I like to read. I write a bit. I love karaoke. I am very nice, very warm, kind, and yes, very sexy. i'm not a gold digger or a slut or a total bitch. My main problem is being overweight seems to be a little bit of a crime these days. No one wants the fat chick . . . sigh. . . . Yes, I am trying to get back in shape, its not always easy. But for now, I seem to have been sent to dating Siberia.

I would like to meet a man btw 30 and 40 who is not completely nuts. Its okay if you are a little weird, who isn't? You should have a job and not be in bankruptcy. You should not have any contagious diseases. You should be warm, you don't have to be that nice cause neither am I. You should have human compassion but also have the ability to laugh at stuff that is uncomfortably funny. Race/religion not important, but I am agnostic and that's all she wrote.

Please have all of or most of your teeth. Hair is optional. You should enjoy art, music, comedy, cooking and be in generally good mood.

I'll tell you what I don't want: I don't want someone who has his apartment decorated with pictures of Tony Soprano and Scarface; I don't want someone who already has a litter of babies and a harem of baby momma's (yuck); if you are in love with yourself—keep moving; if you are constantly in a fit of rage, don't answer my ad . . . please; if you are on more than one type of anti-depressant, that's no good; if you wanna stick it to the man more than once a year . . . eh . . . yeah . . . ; if you are in a constant Model-fucking fantasy even during waking hours, you have come to the wrong place; if you jack off so much you can't orgasm through regular sex, I cannot help you; also, if you only date heavy women because they are so desperate and you are such a perverted bastard that they are the only ones to give you a chance, you too can keep moving on; if you were arrested as early as last year for possession, that is NOT what I am looking for in a man; if you cannot spell or speak proper English, keep moving; if you are looking at a stack of old pizza boxes right now as you read this, get off your butt and clean your apartment; also I am not looking to date the morbidly obese, I am not that much of a mess; if you are one of those crunchy, yoga, tofu, mandala people . . . god, please no; if you must watch soccer every sunday without fail, forget it; I don't care if you watch porno, but if your porno collection is larger than your book collection, thats really sad; if you don't really want a girlfriend and you just want to fuck, do not answer my ad, craigslist has a column for that; no scorpios or pisces please. Jeez, is there anyone left?

Send me your pic, I'll send you mine and let's see what happens. . . . .

—*November 2004,*
www.craigslist.com

I AM THE POSSESSOR of an hereditary domain, and of a castle newly built, situated in a beautiful part of the forests of Bavaria. The castle, which possesses several fine and spacious apartments, is surrounded with lofty mountains, magnificent prairies, fields through the midst of which flow winding streams well adapted for fishing with the line, and forests admirably suited for the chase. This domain lies in a charming valley, where the town of Chant, with its numerous old towers, castles of knights of chivalry, and ancient ruins, awakens in the soul the most poetic souvenirs. But, however delicious this abode may be for those who judge of rural life by the verses of Virgil, Horace, and Delille, I find it too melancholy an idea to consent that any other man but myself should occupy my fine apartments, and admire himself in my splendid mirrors; I have therefore resolved to marry, just like so many other fools: as I am assured that marriages are recorded in heaven, and that it is all a mere lottery, I am anxious to see what heaven has in store for me, and what lovely creature is destined for me by the wheel of fortune.

With this object I submit my views to all young ladies through the medium of the public journals. She whom I would wed must be from 16 to 20 years of age; she must have beautiful hair, handsome teeth, and a charming little foot; she must belong to an honest and good family, and her reputation must be without a stain. She must dress with elegance, but simply. The materials worn by her must be silk and velvet, and no other tissues.

She must not wear earrings, chains, rings, nor any other stupid trinkets of the description; neither must she wear slippers, bonnets, ribands, false hair, &c., nor have her dresses made in the fashion; nothing being more silly than for women to imitate each other as sheep follow the bellwether through a ditch. She must have her robes made to her own taste, and must wear them according to her own fancy, without paying the least attention to what modish ladies may please to say thereanent.

She must know how to ride on horseback, and to drive her own cabriolet, or if she does not, she must learn. She must not under any pretext attempt to knit—a manual occupation, which is the very height of atrocity by which woman have been inspired by her innate stupidity. She must not permit herself the use of music, unless she be perfect in that art, nothing being more disagreeable to those who may come to see you than to be obliged to listen to bad music. She will be absolute mistress at home in all that appertains to domestic affairs, and for my part I shall be most happy to submit to her reasonable caprices, being the declared enemy of passive obedience, and of all submission that resembles slavery, which, thanks to the church, is the source of all quarrels and human discontents.

But she must accompany me in all my journeys and excursions, since woman is, in my opinion, a treasure over which man should watch night and day; and it is by no means proper that he should go to live spendidly in hotels whilst his wife grows weary of her life at home alone. She must not, according to the custom of many households, lose sight of anything that tends to sustain the dignity of woman, nor condescend to be the first to wheedle her husband, as many poor women are found to do, to humour the ill temper of their brutal masters. In making use of the words, "She must do this," and "She must do that," I have not at all intended to subject her to slavery, but to propose to her a contract or convention which may redound to her honour.

On the day of her marriage she shall receive 30,000 florins (upwards of 2,000£ sterling), secured to her either in Russian or Prussian stock, as she pleases, and she will be obliged to spend the interest of this money for her own pleasure, no vice being more abominable than avarice. According to the terms of our convention, she will be forbidden to dance, because I am not at all curious to see my wife jump about like an idiot. If she possesses any property, I do not desire to take it from her when she marries me. She shall dispose of it according to her own good pleasure, as well as of the interest of the money, but under no pretext shall this interest be funding as capital, nothing (as I said before) being more hideous than avarice, and nothing so stupid as to become a treasurer for the benefit of others. The wisdom which regulates my conduct consists in the enjoyment of the pleasures of life and unbroken equanimity.

I should now say something of myself. If I consult my family register, I am a good 70 years of age; but, judging by my health and vigour, I am not more than 25. I am always gay. I seek pleasure everywhere that strict honour permits a man to find it. If there should exist in any quarter a handsome young girl, who likes to ride and travel, or to remain at home with an old husband, who is still robust, gay, and active, she can write to me and I will go to find her, to see her, and to show myself to her, no matter where, provided she is within a radius of 100 leagues from Munich, and not further, engaging upon my honour never to pronounce her name.

Theodore Baron Von Hallberg de Broech, Commander of the Order of St. Michel, Chevalier of the Order of St. Anne, and Captain-Colonel of the Rhine and Meuse. Munich, at the Black Eagle, November 15.

—The Journal of Munich *(Germany)*. *Reprinted January 15, 1841,* The Times *(London)*

MATRIMONIAL—AN AMERICAN gentleman, residing in this City, with an unsullied character and reputation, gently born, good looking, intelligent and refined, warmhearted and domestic, strictly temperate, member of the Episcopal Church, holding a high position, and having a self-support, in the vigor of middle manhood (forty-seven) and still unwedded, adopts this novel method (his lady acquaintances being few and ineligible) of making known his sincere desire to form a matrimonial alliance with a young lady or young widow, without any impediment. She must be respectably connected, of pleasing appearance, good disposition, educated, and refined, and possess some property. Address, with particulars, in good faith, to L.H.B, New York Post Office.

—*August 6, 1860,*
The New York Times

MATRIMONIAL—A YOUNG GENTLEMAN in all respects favorably situated in life, as life is commonly estimated, but still wanting the essential element of happiness; of prepossessing appearance and manners, elevated aims, and he trusts, no ordinary capabilities and attainments, independent in thought and action, enlarged, liberal and charitable in views, to whom all modes (if honorable) are alike, so they achieve the desired end, despising the narrow bigotry and conventionalites of society, which, by interposing barriers to the free intercourse of the sexes, and thus limiting out choices, condemn multitudes of even the most favored to lives of celibacy and misery; regarding the world as his matrimonial field, and believing that it contains somewhere the congenial spirit—the "bright particular star"—the light whose blessed presence and sweet influence his social confines, extensive as contracted souls would consider them, have shut him out from, adopts this method as the only one open to him of testing the reality of his faith and hopes. He made worldly advantages, beyond unquestionable respectability, no condition; but none who, to an agreeable person, expressive face and engaging manners—in short, an attractive tout ensemble externally—do not unite brains and heart (the latter especially) of no common order, need reply; and none such, however high their position, need fear to do so, for their incognitos will of course remain in their own keeping should not a correspondence lead to an acquaintance, in which case the world will be none the wiser as to the means. He is no wife-seeker on easy terms; he intends this for no husband-seekers of the same class, but only for those who, with resources of soul and wealth of affection greater than their opportunities however great, can (at least in an exceptional case, as this claims to be,) rise above the prejudice of mode and tyranny of custom in the search for happiness, and in the hope of escaping the relentless social constriction which crushes out best aspirations within the folds of its "circles" and thus dooms us to become the helpless victims of mere matrimonial chance or accident. Full letters (including description, personal and mental,) solicited, as indicative of character and capacity. Address Bertram, Box No. 152 *Times* Office.

—June 6, 1864,
The New York Times

AN OLD MATRIMONIAL ADVERTISEMENT

Those who believe that the matrimonial advertisement originated with the modem Sunday newspaper should consult the Ipswich Journal of Aug. 21,1802, which contained this advertisement:

TO THE ANGELIC fair of the tree English breed. Worthy notice. Sir John Dinely, of Windsor Castle, recommends himself and his ample fortune to any angelic beauty of a good breed, fit to become and willing to be the mother of a noble heir, and keep up the name of an ancient family ennobled by deeds of arms and ancestral renown. Ladies at a certain period of life need not apply. Fortune favors the bold. Such ladies as this advertisement may induce to apply or send their agents (but no servants or matrons) may direct to me at the Castle, Windsor. Happiness and pleasure are agreeable objects, and should be regarded as well as honor. The lady who shall thus become lay wife will be a baroness and rank accordingly as Lady Dinely of Windsor. Good-will and favor to all ladies of Great Britain. Pull no caps on his account, but favor him with your smiles, and paeans of pleasure await your steps.

Notwithstanding this tempting offer to the fair sex Sir John Dinely died a bachelor in 1808, an inmate of the poor knights' quarters in Windsor castle.

—Aug. 21,1802, Ipswich Journal *(England).*
Reprinted May 27, 1893, Frederick News *(Maryland)*

WANTED BY A middle-aged lady who is good-looking, fine appearing and jolly company, a man who is able and willing to provide a good home and is willing to keep wood and water handy and knows how to lace up a lady's boot and to do housework, which may be required of him, and must be pleasant and agreeable at all times. None other need apply.

—The Advertiser *(Oxford County, Maine).*
Reprinted December, 30, 1901,
Fitchburg Sentinel *(Massachusetts)*

CHAPTER EIGHT

BAD POETRY

SOME FOLKS THINK about the chance to see their words in print and can't resist the urge to rhyme. Poetry has been popping up in personal columns for a long, long time and it doesn't look like the trend will be ending anytime soon. For all their guileless charm, poetic personals can still make a reader cringe.

MECKLA, WELL-BORN, sweet-tempered, bright
and loving
longs for a tender, soft, connubial tie.
She values the strong, manful knight of forty,
far more than the handsomest young dandy.
So faithful would she be to a noble, pure mind,
A truer heart could no Englishman find.

—The Matrimonial News (England).
Reprinted June 21, 1873,
The Denton Journal (Maryland)

LONELY.

IS THERE A lady sufficiently lonely.
—Laughing the laws of convention to scorn,
Who would consent to be onliest only
—Unto a "Gentleman" loving but lorn?
Will she forgive her prospective adorer
—Method of meeting—withholding a frown?
If such a treasure there be I implore her
—Write to "One-twenty-four Herald Downtown."

OBJECT MATRIMONY

Bachelor gentleman, wealthy,
—Income a thousand a week,
Seeks the acquaintance of healthy
—Widow distinguished and chic.
Red rose in bottonhole, Friday at three.
—If I am late kindly tarry for me.

— February 13, 1905,
The Washington Post

"MY NAME IS John and I'm Mr. Right, Please see attached poem!"

My name is John and I'm Mr. Right. I'm looking for a girl that's really out of sight. Her hair is gold and her eyes are green or blue, her heart is caring and her words are true. She loves to live by the golden rule, that's why I find her so very, very cool. I love this girl whose in my mind because to me she's beautiful and always kind. I search for this girl each and every day and I pray to GOD to send me her way. When I find her I'll know she's the one, because whatever we do, it'll be fun. Washing the dishes or a night out on the town, we will be happy and seldom frown. If you've been inspired by the poetry of this man, Please leave your name and number and I'll call you as soon as I can.

—PatheticPersonals.com

The writer of the following poem (we omit a few flourishes) seems in earnest. If any lady wishes to go "out West," the opportunity is now offered.

My dear Mr. Godey, and you, Mrs. Hale,
Will excuse, I am certain, this desecration of the mail,
For I have weighty reasons, as you will find ere I have
   done
Perhaps they fill a bushel, and perhaps they're only one.
When I tell you where I hail from, and I find out what's
   to pay,

Perhaps we'll strike a bargain in our honest merchant
way.
Well, then, out in Missouri there's a snug little
town,
All gravelled, and graded, and macadamized
round,
With plank roads and railroads and rivers a few,
That reach round creation and back again, too;
Perhaps a little incident will bring to mind its
name,
For it ships a pile of bacon and a mighty sight of
grain;
Or, if I have still the vantage, you will find it if you
look
On Uncle Samuel's big map and in Mr. Benton's
book;
'Tis a little west of sunrise and eastward of the hill
Where the Yankees and the Hoosiers their mighty
pockets fill,
With a river just before it and a prairie in the rear,
Where the comets dance the schottish in the winter of
the year.
Now, there many things do happen in this little town of
ours,

Which sets the buck and bachelors a gaping by the
    hours;
And, as I am just midway between those doubtful ages,
I am entitled to the counsels of the editors and sages.
Now, I think, with your assistance, if you make my
    wishes known,
My prospect and appearances are rather good, I own:
I've a snug house in the country, with a hundred acres
    round,
And another in the city of this mighty little town;
And then I have a mule team, a rockaway, and sleigh,
That can beat a steamboat walking in the two and forty
    way;
And these I wish to barter for a requisite of life,
A helpmate and a better half; in other words, a wife.
Now, I am not particular about either form or face,
But would like a pleasing countenance mixed with a
    little grace,
An eye that beams with pleasure, a spirit light and gay
As the winds upon our prairies when the zephyrs are at
    play;
And, if you think there is one would like to come out
    West,

I'll send along the yellow boys by "Adams's Express."
I would add a postscript, also, but this must go to night,
And I hasten to subscribe myself yours.

—Saturday, August 26, 1854,
Godey's Lady Book *(Philadelphia)*
(Courtesy Accessible Archives, www.accessible.com)

CHAPTER NINE

STRAIGHT TO THE POINT

YOU'VE GOT TO admire some personal ads for getting right to the point. Whether their writers are looking for a good tractor or a fine match, the language in this section is plain and honest. Some mention money, titles, or possessions without a hint of hesitation. Others aren't shy when it comes to self-promotion. Whatever the case, these advertisers know exactly what they want and what they have to offer.

WANTED

MIDDLE-AGED WOMAN TO take care of seventy-one-year-old boy.

— *April 18, 1951,*
The Bridgeport Telegram *(Connecticut)*

MONTREAL. I AM an old maid, age 42, weight 119, a Methodist, dark hair, and brown eyes, a substantial beauty, have a house and lot, an orphan, and want some chap to love me.

—*May 14, 1892,*
Canadian Matrimonial News

BRITISH MEN . . . YOU ARE SO YUMMY— 31 (NYC)

I AM COMPLETELY drawn to Brits, especially attractive stylish ones with light eyes. If that's you please send your photo and something about your personality. Please be unattached and serious about getting to know a lovely, attractive, petite American lady for possible LTR.
P.S. This is NOT a post for "marriage of convenience" potential.

— November 2004,
www.craigslist.com

MIDDLE-AGED WIDOWER, tall, good-looking, kind, sympathetic, nice home, sadly needs woman's care; has $30,000; would marry soon. Address Mr. Milton, box 675, Chicago, Ill.

—December 22, 1901,
The Atlanta Constitution

TWO YOUNG LADIES who is wishful to enter the matrimonial state should they be happy enough to meet with respectable partners fortune will be no object provide they could meet with young men possessing the undernamed qualities: good tempered obliging and industrious. Letters post paid, &c

—1828,
The Edinburgh Advertiser *(Scotland)*

MATRIMONIAL: A YOUNG MAN, AGED 19, is desirous of forming the acquaintance of a few young ladies between the ages of 14 and 18. Object—Fun and amusement. Address JAMES SPENCER, Box No. 3787 Post-office.

—November 18, 1865,
The New York Times

WIDOWER—OWNS HOUSE, WISHES to meet
respectable young woman as housekeeper; good
plain cook, with some means, to make a home;
no general delivery answered; confidential; matrimony. Box 844 Free Press.

—August 20, 1920,
Manitoba Free Press *(Canada)*

SWF, 30-SOMETHING wants to be Princess/trophy
wife. Refined but fun. The Plaza/cabin in the
woods! In search of Knight endowing all things
Fairytales are made of. Extra points: great smile,
style, cook. White horse optional. What is your
Fantasy?

—February 18, 2004,
The Austin Chronicle

TWO NEIGHBORLY "literary fellows," 35 and 30, seek social acquaintance of two intelligent, attractive and unconventional young ladies interested in artistic ideas, with a view to mutual improvement and entertainment.

—*1905,* New York Herald.
Ad submitted by William Sydney Porter (more popularly known as O. Henry, the short-story writer)

JUST A GAL seeking her soul mate. SWF 47 relying on two legs and arms on either side of body for balance.

— *April 2004,*
Chicago Reader

SWM, OLD, FAT, balding, many disgusting habits seeks SWF with money. Send pictures of your house, car, RV. This could be your lucky day.

—http://www.lonsberry.com/writers /LBonsberry/index.cfm?story=8025

STRAYED OR STOLEN, my wife, Anna Maria. Whoever returns her will get his head broke. As for trusting her, anybody who can do so who sees fit; for as I never pay any of my own debts, it is not likely that I will lay awake nights thinking of other people's—James Q. Dobson.

—January 24, 1851,
The Times *(London)*

MWM, 52, ISO loving F, under 50. My wife says it's ok for me to have a girl friend as long as she doesn't have to live with her. Let's talk.

— *February 18, 2004,*
Anchorage Press

WANTED: OWNER OF 1940 Buick would like to correspond with widow who has two good tires. Object, Matrimony. Address "Old Bachelor" and please enclose picture of the tires.

—*April 8, 1943,*
The Berkshire Evening Eagle *(Massachusetts)*

WESTERN WIDOW WOULD LIKE TO MEET gentleman to manage ranch; object matrimony. Address RANCH, this office.

—January 28, 1905,
The Washington Post

A BACHELOR OF 40 WOULD LIKE to meet a young lady not over 24 to cook on farm. $20 month; object matrimony; send small photo in first letter; car fare advanced. Box 642, Weyburn, Sask.

—August 3, 1916,
Manitoba Free Press *(Canada)*

FARMER, WIDOWER, Age 47, WANTS to correspond with widow owning farm; object matrimony. Box 2905 Free Press.

—August 11, 1916,
Manitoba Free Press *(Canada)*

TORONTO. I AM tired of being alone musing on pussy and my pug Tansey, want a chubby little woman to love in stead. Am 5 feet 5, and 22.

—May 14, 1892,
Canadian Matrimonial News

PROSPEROUS BUSINESSMAN SEEKS acquaintance of widow or divorcee occupying own flat. Object matrimony. Please send full particulars of flat. Box 703.

—New Delhi newspaper.
Reprinted November 14, 1951,
Traverse City Record-Eagle *(Michigan)*

PERSONAL: BACHELOR WITH 40 acres of excellent land would like to make acquaintance of lady with tractor; matrimony in mind. Please send picture of tractor. Box 325476, Atwater.

—March 5, 1957,
Indiana Evening Gazette *(Pennsylvania)*

THE YOUNG AND highly accomplished daughter of an American millionaire desires to contract an early aristocratic marriage. A title (English if possible) is preferred, but is not essential. Means a secondary consideration, but ancestry is a sine qua non. Ample settlements. Address with editor.

—The Marriage Gazette *(England).*
Reprinted November 1895, The New York Times

MATRIMONY.—AN EARLY but thoroughly aristocratic matrimonial alliance is sought by the attractive and only daughter of an American millionaire, who will respond generously with respect to settlements, in case of a suitable engagement. A British title is preferred, but a distinguished or well-descended foreign nobleman not objected to. Address Ambitions, under cover to Editor, 103, New-Oxford Street, London, W.C.

—The Marriage Gazette *(England).*
Reprinted November 1895, The New York Times

A YOUNG ABLE POLITICIAN, Capable of going to the United States Senate, desires a matrimonial alliance with a young, wealthy lady; a political writer preferred. Address PRESTON FIRMAN, Boston, Mass.

—June 27, 1865,
The New York Times

A GENTLEMAN OF CULTURE and refinement is desirous (for the romance of the affair) of corresponding with a lady who can appreciate a loving disposition and luxuriant home. Lack of money no objection whatsoever, as only a warm, unfettered heart is asked for one as good in return. Address G.D.E. Station D. New York.

—July 17, 1866,
The New York Times

A YOUNG GENTLEMAN of wealth and culture wishes to form the acquaintance of some beautiful and accomplished young lady with a view to matrimony. Address ARTHUR, Box No. 147 Times Office, enclosing photograph.

—November 11, 1869,
The New York Times

MARRIAGES—M. BRUNET, known during a number of years for facilitating marriages, equally advantageous to the two sexes, and whose extensive relations with society, and sound discretion and delicacy, warrant the confidence reposed in him, begs to intimate that there are at present to marry—1. A young lady, aged 22, of a most agreeable countenance, having 300,000 francs; 2. One, aged 20, having 120,000 francs; 3. One, having 150,000 francs; 4. One, having 175,000 francs. Also, three widows, aged 25, 30, and 35, having 10,000, 15,000, and 25,000 francs of yearly income. Apply to M. Brunet, No. 29, Rue de Seine, St. Germain. No letters received unless post paid.

—September 8, 1826,
The Times *(London)*

SUCCESSFUL BUSINESS MAN desires to meet extra large, extremely stout lady, between 30 and 40; object, matrimony; only one who will appreciate unusual comforts and will give full description in first letter need reply. Box 309, this office.

—August 5, 1917,
The Washington Post

WIDOWER, ISRAELITE, 39, large, handsome, with son 14, seeks life companion with means. Would marry into some large undertaking as brewery, mill, grain or cattle business. Widows and guiltless divorcees not excluded.

—German newspaper. Reprinted September 18, 1912, "Odd Ads in German Paper: Those Matrimonially Inclined Frankly State Their Desires in Big Display Type," Evening Post *(Frederick, Maryland)*

REFINED GENTLEMAN OF 36 wishes to correspond with lady from 26 to 30; must be refined
and good housekeeper; correspondence confidential; object matrimony. Address Box 96 Free Press.
Brandon.

—*April 25, 1914,* Morning Free Press
(Winnipeg, Canada)

A MIDDLE-AGED MAN of good character, Norwe-
gian, wishes to meet Scandinavian lady, with view
to matrimony; must have good character. Address
Box 1032 Free Press.

—*April 25, 1914,* Morning Free Press
(Winnipeg, Canada)

GENTLEMAN, 27, MEANS, estate, good character and position, desires to meet lady suitable age. Replies strictly confidential; object matrimony. Box 1181 Free Press.

—*April 25, 1914,* Morning Free Press
(Winnipeg, Canada)

REFINED WEALTHY GENTLEMAN, 32, is desirous of meeting dark young lady of means; object matrimony. Box 2990 Free Press.

—*April 25, 1914,* Morning Free Press
(Winnipeg, Canada)

I WISH TO MAKE the Acquaintance of Lady; Object, Matrimony. For Full Particulars Address E. 4, Care This Office.

—July 26, 1920,
Daily Northwestern *(Oshkosh, Wisconsin)*

YOUNG GENTLEMAN (WHITE) desires to correspond with lady of independent means. Object matrimony. Apply to Romeo, c/o Gleaner.

—May 27, 1920,
Daily Gleaner *(Kingston, Jamaica)*

BACHELOR, 55, EXCEPTIONALLY Educated and Possessed of the Best of Habits, Desires to Correspond With Middle-aged Lady of Refinement; Object, Matrimony. Address P 1, Care of The Northwestern.

—July 7, 1920,
Daily Northwestern *(Oshkosh, Wisconsin)*

A YOUNG MAN residing in Cuba for three years wants to correspond with a young lady, not black, 17 to 22. Education and refinement considered. Must be willing to travel. Object matrimony. Photo and description to F. S. Nuptials, Marcane, Arte. Cuba.

—January 17, 1920,
Daily Gleaner *(Kingston, Jamaica)*

WIDOW, WORTH $65,000 wishes correspondent. Object matrimony. M Box 35. League. Toledo, Ohio.

April 28, 1923,
Middlesboro Daily News *(Kentucky)*

WANTED: STEADY, RELIABLE colored man wants to meet affectionate lady, object matrimony. Write A.Y. McCory, care Jewish Synagogue, Wilson St., Danville, Va.

May 4, 1923,
The Bee *(Danville, Virginia)*

WANTED—I WISH to become acquainted with white woman, object matrimony. Write Sam L. Bearinger, Brushvalley, Pa.

—April 8, 1924,
Indiana Evening Gazette *(Pennsylvania)*

WANTED—ACQUAINTANCE OF widow between 30 and 40 years. No objection to one child. Object matrimony. Write "V." c/o Press.

—January 6, 1923,
Sheboygan Press Telegram *(Wisconsin)*

ATTRACTIVE YOUNG WIDOW, very wealthy but lonesome, wishes to correspond with some nice gentleman. Object matrimony. Address Box 98, Harvey, Ill.

—March 24, 1906,
Iowa City Daily Press

A STEADY, SOBER MAN, with some means; a member of the Christian Church, and not given over to California rowdyism, would like to get acquainted with a good looking lady. Object, matrimony. Triflers need not answer. All correspondence confidential. Address A.B.D., Box 77, Woodland, Cal.

—December 30, 1891,
Woodland Daily Democrat *(California)*

GERMAN 26 YEARS OLD Unacquainted in city, desires to meet sensible girl of German descent (must speak German fluently) to join him in amusement-theater, etc. Gum-chewing kids need not answer; object matrimony. Address O-42. Post-Standard.

—February 16, 1910
Post Standard *(Syracuse, New York)*

YOUNG FARMER WOULD like to make the acquaintance of an honorable young lady of easy-going disposition, not over 25 years of age. Object matrimony, no object as to money or property. All communications confidential. Address L. 10 c/o Daily Press.

—January 3, 1907,
Weekly Press *(St. Joseph, Michigan)*

A MIDDLE AGED WIDOW, very wealthy, nice looking, tired of "single blessedness," wishes to correspond. Lock Box 405, St. Joseph, Michigan.

—September 9, 1906,
Arizona Republican

YOUNG LADY OF MEANS seeking milder climate, wishes gentleman correspondents. Object matrimony. Address J. L. Rich, 235 Washington St., Boston, Mass.

—September 9, 1906,
Arizona Republican

A YOUNG MAN WOULD LIKE to meet lady with ranch or some means. No objections to children. Address W.J., care Republican.

—September 23, 1906,
Arizona Republican

GENTLEMAN, 35 YEARS OLD, wishes to meet a young lady; object matrimony. Address G.P. Reno Gazette.

—March 7, 1907,
Reno Evening Gazette

LADY WISHES TO hear from gentleman with little means; no trifler. Address G. M. Gazette.

—March 7, 1907,
Reno Evening Gazette

A NEW YORK GENTLEMAN of Refinement, means and the highest respectability, desires the acquaintance of a lady equally qualified; object, matrimony. Address H., box 32 station E, New York City.

—November 3, 1869,
New York Herald

MIDDLE-AGED WORKING widower without children, out of town, wishes acquaintance of respectable
lady between 25 and 40; object, matrimony. Address
293, Journal.

—August 22, 1897,
Nebraska State Journal

YOUNG MAN WHO is a stranger in the city would
like to make the acquaintance of young lady;
object, fun. Address 315, Journal.

—August 22, 1897,
Nebraska State Journal

CHARMING YOUNG WIDOW: Independent income; native of Montana; wishes to correspond with upright gentleman; object matrimony. 1310 Brown, Philadelphia.

—February 6, 1901,
Anaconda Standard *(Montana)*

WANTED—YOUNG MAN 37 years of age, good business, desires to meet a young lady of same age, object matrimony. Address John B. Brandt, Nyantotte, Michigan.

—June 26, 1908,
Evening Times *(Cumberland, Maryland)*

MATRIMONIAL ADVERTISEMENT—A lady, young, pretty, bright and poor, desires to make the acquaintance of a man with the opposite qualities, with a view to a happy marriage.

—April 25, 1894,
Davenport Tribune *(Iowa)*

WIDOWER, NO FAMILY, renting a small farm near Kingsbridge, wants a housekeeper; a chapel-going person, and one that has charity, which is the love of God, Preferred; with views of marriage, if the Lord prospers my ways and she be willing.

—British newspaper.
Reprinted October 17, 1907,
Weekly Press *(St. Joseph, Michigan)*

CHAPTER TEN

SELF-DEPRECATING

THESE FOLKS HAVE no money and some of them don't look too great either. But on the good side, they sure are honest.

HELLO, I'M JACK, and I lost everything due to riverboat gambling, and I had a lot to lose. So I'm starting all over again. But it's lonely at the bottom!! Would like to meet someone to talk with and have fun. However must warn ya, I have no money and will not be able to buy dinner, but can cover myself.

—February 17, 2004,
PatheticPersonals.com

WITHOUT BEAUTY TO attract the world's crowd, or gold to allure the fortune hunter, I am, I believe, a true-hearted, refined, educated woman—young, frank, and mirthful, with the birthright entrée of cultured circles—but do not meet with one who fulfills my requirements of mental and moral excellence. Should this reach the eye of any still unwedded, who can prove himself to be truly a gentleman in character and standing, and a man of decided piety, whose aims in life are noble and high, he may, if he wishes, seek correspondence with Miss WARD, No. 946, Broadway, New York.

—December 21, 1859,
The New York Times

I WISH I had a better pic cause that one makes me look like a chalk drawing. (he he) Even makes my face look puffy. To describe myself, I can't say much. People say I'm funny, smart (don't believe them) and I can be outgoing but I need practice. I have trouble meeting people, especially people to hang out with. I've never even been invited to a party. (I hardly know what "party" means unfortunately).

—*February 17, 2004,*
PatheticPersonals.com

ATTRACTIVE WOMAN, not a day over thirty, would be pleased to correspond with eligible man. Not absolutely necessary that he should be young. Would prefer one with property, but one with a good paying position would be satisfactory. The young lady is of medium height, has brown hair and gray eyes, not fat; although most decidedly, she is not skinny. Her friends say she is a fine looking woman. Object matrimony. Reason for this advertisement, the young woman lives in a little dinky town, where the best catches are the boys behind the counters in the dry goods and clothing stores, and every one of them is spoken for by the time he is out of his short pants. Address Hazel Eyes, Box 23. Bingville, Mo. Kansas City Star.

—Kansas City Star. *Reprinted July 22, 1910,* Chicago Herald

CHAPTER ELEVEN

PERSONAL HIJINKS

FOR THE MOST PART, personal ads are filled with earnest folks simply looking for (and finding) an honest lover with whom to share life's journey. However, the personals have always had a reputation for shenanigans. Think that blind date you endured last week was bad? At least you weren't embarrassed, bilked, tricked, or killed.

THE RESULT OF A "PERSONAL"

A FUNNY STORY is told of a lady who was foolish enough to answer a "personal" in a daily paper which stated that a young man was desirous of making the acquaintance of a young women, with a view to matrimony. She carried on a long correspondence with the advertiser, taking, however, the precaution to have her letters copied by a confidential friend. She always sent the copies and retained the originals. Her answers came regularly, but her correspondent was quite as cautious as she was herself, for he always employed a type writer, and she had no means of becoming familiar with his handwriting. Finally, after a good deal of gush, a meeting was agreed upon by the pair, and the lady was somewhat surprised, when she arrived at the place appointed, to see her brother, wearing in his buttonhole the flower which was decided upon as the means of identification. They both acknowledged their folly by indulging in a hearty laugh and went home together, fully resolved to have nothing to do with these traps to catch the unwary, called "personals."

—October 26, 1883,
The Perry Chief *(Iowa)*
(Courtesy www.newspaperarchive.com)

MR. REUBEN LANE walked on crutches from Pennsylvania to Kansas—it took him thirty-six days—only to be turned away when he got there. He was thirty-three, his fiancée, Eliza Ann Parker, was sixty . . . and she turned *him* away on sight.

—*December 22, 1897,*
The New York Times

MRS. BESSIE STINSON of Berlin Falls, N.H., arrived at Neosho Rapids (near Topeka, Kansas) to marry Farmer J.J. Swain. She was "very much disappointed with her prospective husband, and declined to enter into matrimony. Swain was an older man than she expected to see and Mrs. Stinson did not hesitate to express her disappointment by a comparison of his photograph with the gentleman himself." The pair met through an advertisement in a matrimonial paper and she agreed to move to Kansas. The story ended with her "at a neighbor's residence, thinking over the matter."

—*August 1898,*
The New York Times

ADVENTUROUS YOUNG WOMEN have repeatedly, and with unconcealed ambition to be conspicuous, resorted to "globe trotting," but it appears to be reserved for (one) young woman, or a young widow, to indulge in a propensity for travel and incidental mild excitement at the expense of admirers who have never seen her, but who have been prompted to contribute to her desire to see the world by expectations of winning her hand, together with a nugget of fortune alleged to amount to $20,000.

The enterprising young lady, who was pleased to call herself Miss Tillie Marshall, recently appeared in Washington in search of a young man who had been writing to her at San Francisco. The correspondence between the young man, a secretary, and the lady had grown out of an advertisement purporting to be made by a "Young widow with $20,000 matrimonially inclined."

The secretary appears to have been absent when his correspondent visited Washington to find him. But the ubiquitous Sherlock Holmes of the newspaper, who picked up an attractive end of the story, soon discovered that the San Francisco young lady "with $20,000 matrimonially inclined" had been playing tricks with Eastern fortune hunters that might have been learned from the "childlike and bland" Mongolians of One-Eye Alley or Hatchet Lane.

As far as can be learned from the returns now in, at least ten persons who were "willing to wed" the "$20,000 matrimonially inclined" have progressed so far in their fortune hunting as to ascertain the quality of Miss Marshall's penmanship and then to secure, as a very great mark of favor, her photograph. But the "young widow" who calls herself a "Miss" appears to have done better than that; in fact, so well as to raise the presumption that she is a really accomplished widow, able to take care of herself wherever she may chance to be.

The infatuated admirers of this charmer were prevailed upon, either by a desire to win the original of the photograph or the supposed fortune to transmit to her money sufficient to enable her to journey to Chicago, Washington, Philadelphia, and even to New York. The advance of the trifling sum of $150 to $300, even if obtained at a great sacrifice, was a small consideration in view of the loveliness and the fortune to be gained, and a refusal of it, whether unavoidable or prudential, was a final farewell to the "$20,000 matrimonially inclined."

At last accounts this shrewd and bold and possibly beautiful student of human nature had reached Washington, but none of the aspirants to her hand and contributors to the expense of her trip had reached her. If she has any suitors in New York she has afforded them a chance to talk business by announcing that she will stop in this city on her way to Europe, where she intends to pass the Winter as agreeably as the generosity of her admirers will permit.

—September 26, 1897,
The New York Times

IN 1898, THE proprietor of a matrimonial agency in New York City, Mrs Addies Z. DeWitt, was arraigned on a charge of using the mail for fraud. The agency, called "The Exclusive Matrimonial Association," was run out of the East Sixty-fifth street flat shared by Mrs. DeWitt and her husband James. They advertised all over the country. A sample of the advertisements published in Denver follows: *AN AMERICAN LADY, WITH LOVELY*

HOME and $8,000 bank account, longs for congenial, sensible, kind-hearted husband to gladden the sunset of life. Princess, 135, East 65th St., New York. In the same paper, and separated from the foregoing advertisement by only six lines, was the following offer: *WIDOWER. UNENCUMBERED; HIGHEST standing, socially and financially; $200,000; has no congenial lady acquaintance; looks for sensible and devoted wife. "The Judge," 135 East 65th St., New York City.* Among the letters received at the Inspectors' office was one from a correspondent in Denver, inclosing these two advertisements, and saying: "Can't you go to 135 East Sixty-fifth Street and arrange meeting for 'Princess' and 'The Judge?' Being at the same number, some philanthropist ought to introduce them." Because these lonely hearts didn't even exist, Mrs. DeWitt and her husband were playing a dangerous game, collecting money from lonely hearts and giving them little in return.

—*November 4, 1898,*
The New York Times

ADOLF HOCH SPECIALIZED in bilking lonely women over the age of 45. He advertised especially for older women, reported Cynthia Grey, because he found "they were easier to separate from their money."

—1905,
The Sandusky Star Journal *(Ohio)*

MRS. IDA MACOMBER was able to clandestinely place a personal ad in an eastern paper from safe inside a Lincoln, Nebraska, insane asylum. Thousands of letters poured in, many containing money and presents (Mrs. Macomber had claimed in her ad to be the young owner of a ranch worth millions). She attracted the continuing attention of a Mr. Todd of Toledo, an architect who believed she was in prison and continued to correspond despite warnings from the asylum's authorities.

—May 27, 1905,
The Sandusky Star Journal *(Ohio)*

IN THE 1920s, Henry Colin Campbell was seven times a bigamist who met new wives through advertisements and murdered them for their money. A New Yorker who especially sought-out small town women with a desire for big city living, he preyed on the naïve and hopeful. Caught in 1929, he faced a jury trial as the city considered the implications of mail-order romance.

— *June 6, 1929,*
The Sheboygan Press *(Wisconsin)*

A MATRIMONIAL ADVERTISEMENT winds up as follows: "fortune no object, but should require the girl's relation to deposit $10,000 with me as a security for her good behavior."

—*October 31, 1885,*
The Denton Journal *(Maryland)*

GEORGE WILLIAM LUCID, 30, traveler, was found Guilty of defrauding Mary Jackson, a waitress, of £50 by means of a matrimonial advertisement, and Minnie Sutton Cresswell, a cook, of £3 10s. He was also convicted of bigamy Mr. Symmons said the prisoner obtained from a Miss Ransonme, whom he married, £1,500, and having spent the money left her. There were found at his lodgings 2,700 letters from women, mostly referring to money. In 1909 the prisoner was writing to 23 different women; in 1910 to 35, and this year to 42.

—*July 5, 1911,*
The Times *(London)*

IF GULLIBLE, FINE HIM

JUDGE REGRETS HE CANNOT PUNISH VICTIMS OF MATRIMONIAL ADVERTISEMENTS

SPECIAL TO THE NEW YORK TIMES St. Louis, Nov. 4—Judge Dyer of the Federal Court expressed from the bench today his regret that there is no law to punish victims of matrimonial advertisements. He had just fined Mrs. Marion Stire $500 and stayed the sentence when she fainted in the courtroom with a baby in her arms. She was charged with defrauding Michael Nurtaugh and Michael Mallaw out of $90 each when they answered her advertisement for a husband.

—*November 5, 1907,*
The New York Times

TENOR TRAPS AN AUDIENCE

MATRIMONIAL ADVERTISEMENT FILLS A THEATRE FOR HIS DEBUT

PARIS, Dec. 8.—A debut was too important a crisis in the life of Umberto Rota, a young Italian tenor, to leave to chance, so he combined a knowledge of feminine psychology and a talent for publicity to insure a good audience, according to a dispatch from Rome. Recently there appeared in the personal column of a Roman paper an advertisement stating: "Independent man of good appearance and excellent health desires to marry young woman, even if poor. Can be seen Saturday, stage box, Adriano Theatre. (Signed) Umberto Rota." The response left nothing to be desired, but the stage box was unoccupied. On examination of the programs, however, the aspirants recognized in the tenor the prospective fiancé.

—December 9, 1921,
The New York Times

REBEL PERSONAL ADVERTISEMENTS

The following order has just been promulgated: Headquarters Department of the East. New York City, Feb. 5, 1863.

> GENERAL ORDERS No. 10.—Pursuant to instructions from the War Department, notice is hereby given to the editors and proprietors of all newspapers publishing in this department, that the system of correspondence with the rebel States, by advertising under the head of "Personals," or otherwise, in the columns of such papers, must immediately cease. In case the offense be continued, all parties concerned in the publication will be instantly arrested, and brought to immediate trial before a military commission, for violation of the laws of war. By command of Maj. Gen. Din. D.T. Van Buren, Colonel and Assistant Adjutant General. Official: Wright Rives, Captain United States Army, Aid-de-camp.

> —*February 1863,*
> The New York Times

SHOULD A.B. NOT succeed in obtaining the situation required, would that of a housekeeper and companion to a single gentleman, age 30, be likely to suit? He is highly respectable and requires a young lady of cheerful disposition and prepossessing appearance. To one who meets his approval a good salary would be given and a comfortable home. If you think anything of this perhaps you will send full particulars of yourself and also your carte de visite, which shall be returned. Address C.N., 6, Breckneck-place, Camdem-town.

—*March 1864,*
The Times *(London)*

It seems the town's leaders had received the ad in a letter sent by concerned citizens who feared for the purity of their working girls, lured as they might be by this rather innovative pimp. Mr. Alderman Waterlow decided to read the ad out loud in order to bring it to public notice and "give it all the publicity it deserved." —*Editor's Note*

The author of the following advertisement was tried and convicted of murder. —*Editor's Note*

MATRIMONY.—A PRIVATE Gentleman, aged 24, entirely independent, whose disposition is not to be exceeded, has lately lost the chief of his family by the hand of Providence, which has occasioned discord among the remainder, under circumstances most disagreeable to relate. To any female of respectability, who would study for domestic comfort, and willing to confide her future happiness in one every way qualified to render the marriage state desirable, as the advertiser is in affluence; the lady must have the power of some property, which may remain in her own possession. Many very happy marriages have taken place through means similar to this now resorted to, and it is hoped no one will answer this through impertinent curiosity, but should this meet the eye of any agreeable lady, who feels desirous of meeting with a sociable, tender, kind, and sympathetic companion, they will find this advertisement worthy of notice. Honour and secrecy may be relied on. As some little security against all applications, it is requested that letters may be addressed, (post paid) to A.Z. care of Mr. Foster, Stationer, No. 68, Leadenhall Street, which will meet with the most respectful attention.

—*from* An Accurate Account of the
Trial of William Corder

DEFENDING THE PERSONAL AD, 1828

MATRIMONIAL ADVERTISEMENTS WERE not without stigma in their early days. However, they were not without defenders, either. In this fascinating letter to the editor of *Godey's Lady's Book*, a gentleman asserts the efficacy of the personals, thereby paving the way for millions of ad-writing lonely hearts.

LETTER TO THE EDITOR

WE INSERT THE following letter, in the hope that some of our readers will be inclined to reply. The subject is interesting and important, in many respects, and "Coelebs" has stated his case with so much apparent candour, and real good sense, that we think he deserves a hearing in the "Lady's Book."—ED.

> To Mrs. Sarah J. Hale and Miss E. Leslie,
> LADIES,—I have not been a constant reader of your very elegant periodical; which I have to regret, but hope to make amends in future. I lately saw, in the last October number of the "Lady's Book," an article by Mr. MacKenzie, reflecting in the most severe terms upon all advertisements for wives, or for husbands. Mr. M. does not leave a single loop-hole out of which the guilty can escape; he drives them to the wall, and then hews them to pieces. He does not admit that there can be such a combination of circumstances as could, in any event, justify or excuse the act of a gentleman's advertising for a wife, or a lady advertising for a husband. I do not know but that he is perfectly correct; still I can imagine, to say the least, very extenuating circumstances.
>
> I have for a long time thought that the obstacles

in the way of forming matrimonial engagements are much more serious and insurmountable here than are generally supposed. The remark not only applies to this country, but also to every part of Great Britain. "In France, they do these things differently"—there it is never difficult to procure an introduction, with the view to a matrimonial engagement—and it is perfectly comme il faut to avow the object, and even to employ a person to call on the friends of the lady, or her parents, and make the proposal. In this country, nothing of that kind is permitted; and although a gentleman may live for years next door to the residence of a lady, yet he cannot be allowed to make any approaches to her, unless acquainted with her friends, or introduced altogether, as it were, by accident; nor is the lady, how much soever she may desire it, ever allowed to make the least advances. Now I am disposed to think that there may be a fault in all this, and that in every country, there should exist some honourable medium of communication.

This state of things with us, bears very severely upon the higher classes of unmarried ladies, and the same class of gentlemen: now if a lady does not meet a gentleman in her immediate set, or clique of society, with whom she is pleased, and this must be reciprocal, why, she must fold up her hands and remain for ever single, how much soever she may desire the happiness of matrimonial life. It is this which fills our large cities, in all the upper classes of society, with old maids. This same state of things, operates with the greatest severity upon the fate and fortunes of great numbers of gentlemen, whose education, habits, and tastes, would fit them to adorn any station in society. Accident, or the caprices of fashion, or a want of acquaintances, or the means of making them, very frequently, yes, in thousands of instances, compel such gentlemen, either to form unsuitable and unhappy alliances, or remain for ever single. This is true, not only with regard to numbers who do not boast of great wealth, but also with the richest individuals in the community. All of your readers must recollect the happy termination of a proposal made at a wedding party in South Carolina, that each lady should write on a piece of paper, the name of any gentleman present, whom she would consent to have; and vice versa, the gentleman should also write the name of the lady whom he should fancy. These sealed papers, given to the president, and parties reciprocal through him received the pleasant intelligence:—nine marriages resulted from this plan, in a party of fourteen couple, and many of the gentlemen afterwards declared, that they should not have had the courage to address the ladies, unless through this happy suggestion.

In the middling and less aspiring, and less fashionable classes of society, nearly all persons marry, but the moment we begin to ascend the scale of society, and approach the opulent or ambitious, we find numbers who never marry. How often it is, that a young lady, a minor or ward, possessed of property, is completely surrounded by interested keepers, who prevent all approaches to her, as assiduously and completely, as if she were enclosed in the walls of a harem. I will not dwell on this unpleasant part of the subject, but will only remark, that nine-tenths of runaway matches, arise from this imprisoned condition of the lady. I have known several unhappy instances of this sort, which could not have taken place, had there been a little more latitude permitted in the conventional rules of society.

But the ladies may relate their own sad tales;— my especial business is with the gentlemen; and to prevent all mistakes or misrepresentation, I will tell my own tale as an exemplification of my previous remarks. I am a bachelor, about thirty-two years of age, possessed of a respectable fortune, amounting to some thousands of dollars annual income. My religious habits from very early life, have led me to avoid the gay circles of society; and on the other hand, my abhorrence of cant, and ultra religion, have prevented me from very close connection with religious circles of society, who at the best, have very limited correspondence, or social relation with each other; the consequence is, that I am entirely out of society; have many male acquaintances, and but very few female— have a great attachment for ladies; and am a very ardent admirer of the female character. My education is rather of a high order.

I have long desired to enter in the matrimonial state, but begin to fear that such will never be my lot; and I will tell you the kind of lady I would prefer:—the lady I would wish to be between twenty and thirty years of age, rather handsome than decidedly ugly; and above, rather than greatly below the middling height; and possessed of a respectable fortune. Now these three conditions I consider as bagatelles, compared with the following, which are, a first rate, and accomplished education, pure piety, and of respectable family. These are my wishes, and this is my ambition; yet I cannot gratify it—I find it to me, impossible. I am not alone—I have two intimate friends, who are situated like myself, possessing education, talents, personal respectability, and wealth, and yet find it impossible, in the circle of their acquaintance, to meet with ladies of such character and qualifications, as they would select for matrimonial partners.

Now, I would ask the question, if gentlemen, under these circumstances, who greatly desire matrimony, cannot be excused if they were to take, what among us are considered extraordinary measures, even to an advertisement in the public papers? I should like to hear your opinion upon these subjects, or that of some of your fair correspondents. I have heard much opprobrium cast upon bachelors for being so, and yet in an extensive acquaintance, both in this country and in Europe, I never heard a bachelor express himself satisfied with celibacy, but rather regret, and often with the keenest sensibility, that a kind Providence should have ordained them to a single life; and if by any hint, or remark, or suggestion, you can put me and my friends in the way of reaching the goal of our earthly hopes, we should ever owe you a debt of the deepest gratitude. Respectfully yours, COELEBS.

—Godey's Lady's Book *(Philadelphia)*
(Courtesy Accessible Archives, www.accessible.com)

The letter above was written in response to the following incendiary missive:

WIVES BY ADVERTISEMENT
BY R. SHELTON MACKENZIE

THERE ARE MANY wretched persons—miserable in mind and in prospect—poor in pocket and in spirit—unhappy by reason of their own doings, or the deeds of others: for such there is pity, and there may be pardon. But there is a class yet lower, almost beneath contempt, who are the artificers of their own shame. In this motley world, among those classes who rank as the "civilized," there is one set of persons sunk in abasement and wretchedness far, far beneath the vicious or the pauper,—those are the men who advertise for wives!

The lowest creature upon earth,—lower far than the beggar whose rags float in the wind, and whose bed is in the ditch by the way-side, is the wretched one who advertises for a wife. His doing so is an open and undisguised avowal of his own great unworthiness. It proclaims that he is unable or unworthy to obtain a wife by the usual means. His vices may have shut him out from reputable female society; his defects of mind or person,— perhaps both,—may have excluded him from being known to the respectable portion of wom-ankind, for not otherwise can any man lack the means of being introduced to the acquaintance of women of character. Thus isolated, he puts him-self up to the public bidding, for the unworthy to purchase. He proclaims that he is in the market, like any other commodity. He avows that pride, passion, principle, are all abandoned; he only wants to wed for money. Is there any creature more debased than such a thing?

The advertiser usually (indeed, almost invari-ably, for as yet the fair sex are not quite so self-degraded) is a male. By his own account, he is young, wealthy, and accomplished. Is it not passing strange that such a gifted being is so utterly unacquainted with reputable females, as to be compelled to put himself up to public bidding? To render himself the laughed-at dupe of all who may select him as the butt for their covert mockeries? To degrade the name of man—to defame the fair character of woman—to disgrace marriage (a sacrament of one church and a holy ordinance of all), by avowing himself purchasable by any female who may be hopeless enough to make such a bargain—heartless enough to put up with it? Who can—who must be the repliers to such an advertisement? The old, the ill-favoured, the unprincipled, the characterless; all whose demerits have not enabled them to get a husband before.

The woman who seriously replies to such an advertisement must have abandoned all sense of the touching, beautiful, and becoming delicacy of her sex. There must be a deliberate resolve to discard that modesty which is the brightest gem that female decorum can wear, to prostrate her mind and curb her feelings,—to level herself to the utter degradation which such a negotiation involves; for, besides the bold assurance requisite for such bargaining with an utter stranger, the poor wretch must have made up her mind to the chance of being refused. The advertiser may be a little fastidious, and disapprove of her; a little capricious, and reject her; or a little facetious, and have been only playing a trick.

After a long courtship, conducted with respect on one side and modesty on the other, a delicate minded maiden in private life hesitates to say "Yes" to the hearted request of her affectionate, her faithful, her long-tried lover: but here the position is reversed. The heartless female may hear a refusal from the lips of the stranger with whom she has been bargaining for marriage! What humiliation for a woman.

Bankrupt, indeed, in charms and character must she be who would proffer herself as the spouse of a wife-advertiser for the fulfillment of such a speculation. What can they expect from a union thus composed of the mingled elements of all that is wretched in mind and base in purpose? Seek they for love? It is a holy passion, not to be told nor bought. Strive they for happiness? Chat, also, is not a marketable article. Hope they to meet with the esteem of each other? Alas! they cannot have their own! All sympathy of taste, all mutuality of feeling, all congeniality of temper, all the charms and all the decencies of the marriage state, they must take on hearsay. They buy each other, as we buy cattle. Their qualifications must be discounted in the bargain. They cannot love: theirs is a contract from which delicacy shrinks, and at which pride revolts. If they should have children, with what face can they tell them that they, the parents, became wedded through the introduction of a newspaper advertisement. That man should be so fallen, and that woman should be so mean, as to be linked together by such ties, is one of the marvels to which the venality of this buying and selling age has unhappily given birth. That eminent individual, Mr. William Corder (who happened to get hanged one day, in Suffolk, for the murder of a young woman whom he seduced), obtained a wife by an advertisement in a London paper. A very pretty precedent for such delicately-minded ladies and gentlemen!

Think, also, on the chance of the husband's being tricked. He may be deceived in the amount of the "value received" for his precious person. Instead of opulence, he may have become wedded to poverty; instead of luxuriously living in wealth and splendour, he may have espoused one deeply in debt, who by her marriage provides herself with a scape-goat, to rot in the prison, which otherwise would have received herself; for it is part of the English law, that the husband is accountable, in purse or person, for the previous debts of the wife.

What a sweet cat-and-dog sort of union must that be, where mutual confidence cannot exist. It is a desecration of marriage. It is the abuse of the ordinances of religion to legalize prostitution of mind and body. It degrades marriage to mere animal sensuality. It tears the veil from the sanctity of that state which has something higher and holier than mere passion for its impulse: something of a mind to delight in and repose on, when the edge of appetite is dulled. It is, in a word, a disgrace to the social compact, in a Christian land, that a man should openly put himself up to the heartless bidding of wealth, and sell himself for gold.

From such marriages the prospect of felicity is small. Love must be quite out of the question. How can the man love her who buys him? How can the woman esteem him who not only marries her for money, but must have some extraordinary deficiencies to preclude him from obtaining an introduction to female society, from which he might select a wife in the usual and legitimate manner? Wretchedly low must be the man or the woman who is content to take a wife or husband on trust.

The infection has crossed the waters. Matrimonial advertisements frequently appear in American papers, as well as in Paris papers. There are but few female advertisers in either country—though they are numerous in France; but this arises, not from modesty (because whoever would answer such an advertisement would advertise), but because men are not yet quite so abandoned as to accept a lady who offers herself.

Of the two, the male advertiser is the more degraded; he abandons himself to the indiscriminate biddings (the term is a marked one) of the females, and resigns his privilege of choosing and asking a wife for himself. Even in India, whither English belles resort on matrimonial speculations, they pass through the ordinary ordeal of private introduction, they must be seen before the negotiation for them commences, and the man does not blindly run himself into the matrimonial halter. The advertiser may lose his chance. He may be content to risk his prospect of future happiness upon, perhaps, one interview: the lady may be virtuous (the chances being forty to one that she is not), but may be she is not equally vicious! The only consoling prospect is, that when he has spent his spouse's fortune, he can take the wings of the next packet-ship and cross the "deep, deep sea,'" leaving the dama to despair, and the chance of another advertisement. Could she expect constancy—or love—or confidence—or respect?

It is worth consideration, that, in almost every instance, the wife-advertiser puts in the interesting inuendo, that the lady "must have some property," which, he modestly intimates, "may be settled upon herself." Kind hearted wife-seeker! he will be moderately content to live upon the interest of her fortune.

The impudence of these announcements is extraordinary. One, now before me, states that a wife is wanted (with a good fortune), and ending with the very encouraging hint, that "to a lady whose mental acquirements would render the unemployed hours of the advertiser agreeable, a preference would be given." Think of that, Master Brooke! "a preference would be given!"—it is the languages of an auctioneer when he advertises property for sale.

The matter is this—that the advertisement puts the man up to female competition. Are women indeed so badly off that they must seek husbands?

If the advertiser should find a purchaser, let

the buyer and the bought have the curse of remembering, for ever, that one has paid money for a husband for her pruriency; the other sold himself as a slave, for a daily dole of food, and a decent coat.

Better break stones by the highway—better beg—better starve—than thus degrade the dignity of manhood.

—Godey's Lady's Book *(Philadelphia)*
(Courtesy Accessible Archives, www.accessible.com)

ACKNOWLEDGMENTS

THANKS TO MY PARENTS, Linda and Michael Artz and Michael Schaefer, for their love and encouragement.

Thank you to Aimee Tritt, Brett Mobbs, and Karen Meyer.

Thanks to the Wisconsin Historical Society and their wonderful Madison library. A huge debt of gratitude to Newspaper-Archive.com, an amazing resource. Thanks also to Accessible Archives and PatheticPersonals.com.

Finally, a big thanks to my literary manager, Scott Hoffman, and my editor, Catheline Jean-François.